Uplifting Encouragement For The Soul

31 Day Journey to the Promises of God

Dr. Bendetta Perry

Uplifting Encouragement for the Soul

31 Day Journey to the Promises of God
Written by Dr. Bendetta Perry

For Speaking Engagements or request to reproduce this publication, contact the author: Dr. Bendetta Perry at: fruitfulministry@hotmail.com

Book completion services provided by
TRU Statement Publications
www.trustatementpublications.com

First Printing: 2019

ISBN-13: 978-1-948085-28-1

Dedication

I dedicate this book to God, my Lord and Savior. Without the Holy Spirit as my guide, I would have never been able to pick up the pen and write the words on these pages.

I dedicate this book to my son, Je'Marc, and his wife, Tomesha, all their family, along with my joyful granddaughter, Jaelah, who brightens up a room with her excitement and love for life; also to my son Andrae, and my granddaughter, Ariyah, who has grown up to be an awesome young lady, who believes God at His word; I pray that as you all take the 31-day journey through this book, you will know there is a God Promise to every situation that we face, and God allows each of us to see the rainbow.

To my brother, Duane Hampton, and my sister-in-love, Pamela Hampton, and their two children,

Brandon and Janelle, my sister, Denise Nimons, and her three children, Deleon, and wife Vita, and my two nieces, DeAudrey and Aria; I love you family, we may be small in number, but we have a big heart of love for one another. I pray that each of God's promises, that you claim on this 31-day journey, will manifest as a blessing in each of your lives.

To my parents, Mr. Thirkee and Alice Hampton, thank you for loving me and taking care of our family with limited income and education. You both worked hard without one complaint. You finished your journey well. Rejoice in Heaven.

To all who may be in need of encouragement, or know of someone who may be stuck in the time zone of their past and who cannot seem to press forward, I encourage you to take this 31 Day Journey, "Uplifting Encouragement for The Soul."

Forward by
Dr. Curtis Dodson

Well, here we go again. Dr. Bendetta Perry is once again demonstrating her profound God given ability to connect with her audience through the medium of words.

This woman has taken her life's experiences and that of others, packaged them into a bundle of hope and healing for the rest of us.

Known for her dramatic presentations and "Fragrance of The Spirit Ministries, we have come to expect whatever has her name is on, it has already been signed and sealed by God. I highly recommend this book to everyone looking for a word of hope and encouragement.

Dr. Curtis Dodson,
Founder of Word Wise Ministries

Forward by
Rev./Evangelist Beverly Benton

Although there are other books out there which speaks about giving "Uplift and Encouragement," there is not one to compare with this book; it speaks to the depths of your soul. This book will stir your soul, emotions, and your mind in a way no book has ever done. *"Uplifting Encouragement for the Soul,"* A 31 Day Journey to the Promises of God.

Evangelist Bendetta Perry, for over a decade, has been writing to encourage herself and others from her victorious life experiences; even through, the sudden death of her dear husband, and life's challenges.

Evangelist Bendetta Perry is an anointed woman of God, a sought-after gifted preacher, whom I respect and honor, is touching the human soul through these writings, poems, and preaching's. She is a blessing to the Body of Christ. You will be uplifted, refreshed, revived, encouraged, and changed by reading this inspirational book.

In light of life's many disappointments, ups and downs, and lonely moments, people are looking for encouragement to get through a day or the week. Evangelist Perry understands this, and knows God is using these powerful spiritual writings and poems to encourage and empower everyone who reads this book.

Rev./Evangelist Beverly Benton,
Founder and Visionary
Christian Women's Devotional Alliance
Women of Strength, Courage & Diversity
California Clergy Girls Connections
Community Outreach Women's & Girls Alliance

Acknowledgement

Thank you, to all my family and friends. I love and appreciate you all for your love, support, and believing in me. In good times and bad times, you all have been by my side, for evermore, with your unconditional love.

Thank you, to my Spiritual covering and Pastor, Dr. Apostle Jarvis and First Lady Vanessa Hines, of Consuming Fire Ministries International. I praise God for you both, covering me and acknowledging the gifts that God placed within me for the Kingdom, to reach the world for Christ. Thank you both, for being the vessels that God uses to flow His love and power through. Love you both.

Thank you to my special friends Debra Whiteside, Lilly Cooper, Melody Menal, Antoinette Sims, Rosetta Love, Shayanna Washington, Lula

Dickson, and Merlie Huey, who has always supported me in ministry.

Thank you to my co-workers in Christ:

Dr. Vicki Pichon, of GWOW (God's Women of the Word), for your support of me and all women in ministry, for allowing me and countless others to grace your platform ministering the Word of God.

Minister Mandy Miranda Salazar, of The Platform Ministry, for giving all ladies the opportunity to move in their gifts and talents, and the pleasure of working with you as we perform theatrical biblical characters from the bible.

Pastor Susan Flores, Founder of the Love Ministries (*Ladies of Virtue and Edification Ministries*), who has poured out countless seeds of love, encouragement, and guidance into the lives of many ministries and others who are in need.

Melinda Cuellar, Founder of Divine Connections and Hope, After Domestic Violence Ministry, for your encouraging words, support, and love to women who have been victims of domestic violence.

Dr. Roseanna Campos, Founder of W.O.W.W. (*Woman of Worship and Warfare*), for teaching all women how to War in the Spirit.

Apostle Cathy Coppola, Founder of Cathy Coppola International Ministries, who sets the captive free with her powerful teaching, *When the power of God invades the power of darkness, miracles happen.*

Dr. Trudy Coleman, Founder of JEMTA (*Juneteenth Education Technology Mobile Arts Center, Inc*), "Teaching Today, Tomorrow's Leaders." Thank you for allowing me to speak at your yearly events, it is always a pleasure and honor.

Introductions

I remember being overwhelmed after the death of my husband. In my grief and mourning, I wrote a recipe to help me not give up on my dreams. My recipe is about abounding in perseverance, determination, conquering my fears through prayer, renewing my mind by reading God's Word, becoming dedicated, forgiving my past failures, embracing the freedom to dream, and accepting my future, with optimism and hope. This same recipe will work for you.

Thus, this inspiration births forth this book. This book is an inspiring mixture of sermons, spoken word, and testimonies. Within these pages are breaths of life empowering your body, spirit, and soul inspired by the Word of God.

Beloved, you are God's Diamond, Ruby, Pearl, and other precious jewels in His sight. God wants you to remember that you are valuable to Him. You are an inspiration, revitalization, and a resource for words of encouragement. Knowing your worth is greater than a gift of gold.

We all battle moments of depression, anxiety, fear, low self-esteem, self-doubt, insecurity, hopelessness, loneliness, tragedy, and devastation. In those seasons, I chose to write words of encouragement that I share in the following pages. My intent is to inspire each reader to know, regardless of whatever you are going through, you have a pre-ordained destiny of which you were created to fulfill.

Live on and strive beyond the storms of life. Journey towards the promises of God, which release sunshine and a heavenly rainbow filled with sunny days.

Uplifting Encouragement for the Soul
Definitions

UPLIFTING

Spiritually elevating; and inspiring.

ENCOUAGMENT

The act of giving someone support, confidence, or hope by offering positive words. Within the word encouragement we see the word "courage," which means the ability to face danger and deal with it.

SOUL

Mind, will, intellect and emotions.

Order of Articles

Focus is

completion

of your assignment.

~Dr. Bendetta Perry

Day 1

Recipe for Pressing Forward and Unlimited Measurements

Ingredients

1. *Perseverance*
2. *Determination*
3. *Conquering Your Fears*
4. *Renewed Mind*
5. *Dedication*
6. *Forgiving Past Failures*
7. *Freedom to Dream*
8. *Embracing Your Future*

Directions

With a hungry appetite to succeed, bring all the ingredients before you; and with no limits, measure each ingredient one-step at a time and stir them into your life.

Soon, you will feel a rising within the depths of your spirit that will cause you to push, push, and push towards your future.

Finally, the sweet aroma of God's promise of good success is upon your life; making you an example to friends, family and associates. God is glorified through your press and commitment to His word. Now release the savor of Success!

<u>Prayer</u>

Thank you, Lord, for choosing and giving me the strength that I need in my life, and for the press. Now, use me Lord to encourage someone else to push, push, and push towards their future.

God's Promise for You Today
(Meditate)

Proverbs 16:3 (NIV)

"Commit to the Lord whatever you do, and he will establish your plans."

Joshua 1:8 (NHEB)

"This book of the law shall not depart out of your mouth, but you shall meditate on it day and night, that you may observe to do according to all that is written therein: for then you shall make your way prosperous, and they you shall have good success."

Philippians 4:13 (NKJV)

"I can do all things through Christ who strengthens me."

Journal Your Journey

Start your day with a new recipe for success. Apply the ingredients to your life today, and throughout the day, reflect and journal your results.

_____

_____

_____

_____

_____

_____

_____

_____

_____

_____

_____

_____

_____

_____

_____

_____

_____

_____

_____

_____

_____

_____

_____

_____

_____

_____

_____

_____

_____

_____

_____

_____

_____

_____

_____

_____

_____

For opportunities to succeed, you must Rebound!

~Dr. Bendetta Perry

Day 2

Rebound, You Are Still in The Game!

*L*ife is a process of events: survival, character development, opportunities, continual change, and victory or defeat. Many people refer to our lives as, *"Winning the game of life,"* by achieving their goals. Life may hit you hard with its unexpected disappointments, twists, and turns. While traveling through the journey of life, we cannot afford to become stuck in a time zone every time we have a defeat in life that hits us hard.

I had to learn how to rebound (*bounce back*) from the death of a spouse, misunderstandings between friends, church hurt, sickness, financial hardships, and no transportation by taking another shot on the court yard of life and confessing God's Word in Isaiah 54:17, *"No weapon formed against me shall prosper, and every tongue that rises against me in judgment God shall condemn it."*

We all have times of failure and mistakes in our lives. Experiencing a lack of success, after putting all effort towards winning, can be devastating. Watching basketball games have taught me that what is more important than getting the ball in the basket, is when you miss the basket and catch the rebound. The passage in the bible Proverbs 24:16 says, *"A just man falls seven times and rises up again."*

Peter and the disciples were professional fishermen who caught fish for a living. The disciple worked hard all night and caught nothing.

Later, Jesus instructed the disciples to go into the deep waters and let down the nets to catch (to take the shot again). The fishermen followed Jesus' exact instructions in book of Luke 5:3-8, *"He (Jesus) said to Simon (Peter), 'Put out into deep water, and let down the nets for a catch.' Simeon answered, 'Master, we've worked hard all night and haven't caught anything. But because you say so, I will let down the nets."*

When they had done so, they caught such a large number of fish that their nets began to break. So, they signaled their partners in the other boat to come and help them, and they came and filled both boats, so full, that they began to sink.

This is a clear example of the blessing of overflow, which is the signature hand of God's favor on your life when you are obedient to His instructions, in the Word of God. The true mark of your success is not that you've fallen; it is that you rebound, took another shot, and got back in the game of life.

<u>God's Promise for You Today</u>
(Meditate)

Ephesians 3:20-21 (KJV)

"Now to Him who is able to do exceedingly abundantly above all that we ask or think, according to the power that works in us."

Isaiah 41:13 (NIV)

"For I am the LORD your God who takes hold of your right hand and says to you, do not fear, I will help you."

Proverbs 24:16 (NKJV)

"For a righteous man may fall seven times and rise again, but the wicked shall fall by calamity."

Journal Your Journey

Recall a times in your life when you missed the shot, and believed you were facing defeat, but it all turned around because you faithfully followed God and caught the rebound.

Day 2
Rebound, You Are Still in The Game!

_____

_____

_____

_____

_____

_____

_____

_____

_____

_____

_____

_____

_____

_____

_____

_____

_____

_____

_____

_____

_____

_____

_____

_____

_____

_____

_____

_____

_____

_____

_____

_____

_____

_____

_____

_____

_____

_____

_____

_____

_____

_____

_____

_____

_____

_____

_____

_____

_____

_____

_____

_____

_____

_____

_____

_____

_____

_____

_____

_____

The comfort zone is a delightful place, but nothing ever grows there. Time to leave the Comfort Zone!

~Dr. Bendetta Perry

Day 3

Inspired Change

When is Change Inspired?

In every change of season, winter, spring, summer, and fall, God provides the necessary conditions that inspire the production and growth of the fruit that sustains life on earth. Within each of us, fruit must be produced and grow to sustain us, and for those we encounter.

Change in our lives is like the seasons of the earth. They are inspired by God to help shape, mold, and develop us to fulfill the purpose for which we were created; like the metamorphosis of the butterfly which goes through four stages: egg, larva, pupa and adult.

Stage One: Eggs are laid on top of a milkweed plant and takes about four days to hatch.

Stage Two: Caterpillar or feeding stage of the butterfly is when the body is wormlike and eats lots of plants for development, and this lasts about 10 to 14 days.

Stage Three: Pupa or transition stage is when the caterpillar is full grown. The old body of the caterpillar dies, and a new body is formed inside the protective shell for 10 to 14 days.

Stage Four: Adult is when the pupa opens up. Soon a butterfly comes out.

Butterflies are beautiful and very colorful. Each stage is inspired by God and had a different goal. Now is the season for the butterfly to fly and touch the sky.

Do not fear change but accept it. You are God's amazing masterpiece. You are being formed daily and are transforming into a beautiful image of Him.

Embrace every season knowing that God has Inspired your Change!

<u>God's Promise for You Today</u>
(Meditate)

Ecclesiastes 3:1 (KJV)

"To everything there is a season, and a time to every purpose under the heaven."

Isaiah 43:19 (KJV)

"Behold, I will do a new thing; now it shall spring forth; shall you not know it? I will even make a way in the wilderness, and rivers in the desert."

Isaiah 40:31 (KJV)

"But they that wait upon the LORD shall renew their strength, they shall mount up with wings like eagles; they shall run and not be weary, they shall walk and not faint."

Journal Your Journey

Compare your process of change to the maturation of the butterfly. Identify your current stage and journal the details of what this process looks like and what changes you have encountered.

_____

_____

_____

_____

_____

_____

_____

_____

_____

_____

_____

_____

_____

_____

_____

_____

_____

_____

_____

_____

_____

_____

_____

_____

_____

_____

_____

_____

_____

_____

_____

_____

_____

_____

_____

_____

_____

_____

_____

_____

_____

_____

_____

_____

_____

_____

_____

_____

_____

_____

_____

_____

_____

_____

_____

_____

_____

_____

Traveling through
the Journey of Life
and not chained to
the Time Zones.

~Dr. Bendetta Perry

Day 4

Life Traveler's

Time Zones

Traveling through life's journey with many paths to choose and decisions to make; some wise and unwise, yet not chained in the time zones. For each journey traveled, leads to the transformation of our lives; forgetting past failures and reaching the highest goals.

The Accomplishment of that we Aim For!

*D*eliverance does not come easy. Months and years can be spent trying to recover, and recovery is not always guaranteed. Getting detoured and lost in life can happen overnight. All it takes is a traumatic experience early on or even later in life, and poof, depression, drugs, promiscuity, bankrupt, poverty, or domestic violence can grip you with no end in sight. But thanks to the Kingdom of God, and the power of His dear son, Jesus the Messiah, deliverance can be had.

All too often, both women and men fall to circumstances, but God can deliver. Situations can start early in life. All it takes is a bath given by the wrong person and your whole life gets turned upside down. To make matters worse, a mother not believing her child over a mate can send the child into a downward spiral; and only bad behavior can keep them from drowning, which in turns perpetuates the situation.

Can you recover your life from the ashes of despair?

Yes!

Through the grace of God, there are many in general and a few I know in particular, who have broken the chains of bondage, turned their lives around, and are living victoriously.

A little girl, bathed by the mother's boyfriend, turned to a life of promiscuity, drugs, depression, and prostitution. Hitting rock bottom with no place to go but up, cried out to the Father for help. Praise be, God heard and helped.

In so many cases of similar situations, that little girl became the woman of her dreams and is now living the life of personal, academic, and financial success. With you and God, as a team, there is nothing you can't overcome.

<u>*God's Promise for You Today*</u>
(Meditate)

Isaiah 41:10 (NIV)

"So do not fear, for I am with you; do not be dismayed, for I am your God. I will strengthen you and help you; I will uphold you, with my righteous hand."

Psalm 147:3 (NIV)

"He heals the brokenhearted and binds up their wounds."

1 Corinthians 10:13 (NIV)

"No temptation has overtaken you except what is common to mankind. And God is faithful; he will not let you be tempted beyond what you can bear. But when you are tempted, he will also provide a way out so that you can endure."

Journal Your Journey

Are you a Life's Traveler? What have you overcome with the help of God? How have you turned your ashes of despair, into the beauty of hope?

Day 4
Life Traveler's

_____

_____

_____

_____

_____

_____

_____

_____

_____

_____

_____

_____

_____

_____

_____

_____

_____

_____

_____

_____

_____

_____

_____

_____

_____

_____

_____

_____

_____

_____

_____

_____

_____

_____

_____

_____

_____

_____

_____

She releases the aroma of Victory as her Perfume!

~Dr. Bendetta Perry

Day 5

Who is She?

She *loved.*

She *hurt.*

She *cried.*

She *laughed.*

She *made mistakes.*

She *raised children.*

She *became distracted with life.*

She *fell down.*

She *got back up.*

She *turned her dreams into Reality.*

She *turned her failures into Victories.*

She *answered the call of God on her life.*

Who is *She?*

She is every woman that ever had an obstacle and overcame by obtaining Victory.

She Is You and I!

God's Promise for You Today
(Meditate)

Proverbs 31:25 (NIV)

"She is clothed with strength and dignity; she can laugh at the days to come."

Psalm 46:5 (NIV)

"God is within her, she will not fail, God will help her at break of day."

Esther 4: 15-16 (NIV)

"Then Esther send this reply to Mordecai: Go, gather together all the Jews who are in Susa, and fast for me. Do not eat or drink for three days, night or day. I and my attendants will fast as you do. When this is done. I will go to the King, even though it is against the law. And if I perish, I perish."

Journal Your Journey

Write your own affirmation of who you are. Who are you in the eyes of our heavenly Father, and who are you in the eyes of those who love and depend on you? They know who you are, do you?

_____

_____

_____

_____

_____

_____

_____

_____

_____

_____

_____

_____

_____

_____

_____

_____

_____

_____

Success is looking for You. Just like You are looking for Success. The two of you will connect. Speak It!

~Dr. Bendetta Perry

Day 6

Death and Life is in The Tongue Speak It!

*W*e can use our tongue to bring blessings and life or curses and death. Words can hurt and bring death to situations that should be a blessing. There is hope; the bible tells us that with the help of the Holy Spirit, we can have power and control over our tongue and bring life to a dead situation.

Many times, people have found themselves in a despondent situation and instead of speaking life and aspiration over their circumstances, by allowing God to turn it around for His glory, they speak hopeless words of negativity and doom.

In the bible, there was a man name Jabez whose name meant sorrow. His mother said, *"Because I bored him with pain, your name was your destiny, for it related to who you were to become."*

Jabez changed what his mother had spoken over his life by praying in 2 Chronicles 4:10, *"And*

Jabez, called on the God of Israel saying, Oh that you would bless me indeed, and enlarge my territory, that your hand would be with me, and that you would keep me from evil, that I may not cause pain, so God granted him what he requested."

Death and life are in the power of your tongue, words, and power of speech. Speak life in abundance over yourself, family, friends, and circumstances. Psalm 118:17 says, *"I shall not die, but live, and declare the works of the Lord."*

Jairus, one of the rulers of the synagogue, had a little girl about 12 years old. She was sick and Jairus wanted Jesus to go to her and pray for the healing of her body. When Jesus arrives at the home, He saw mourners crying saying the child is dead. Jesus spoke life to the mourners, He said to them, *"Why make this commotion and weep, the child is not dead but sleeping."*

They laughed at him to scorn and Jesus put them all out, just as the Lord put out all doubt, unbelief, fear, negative words, or laughing, and speaks life over that which is dead in your life.

Jesus spoke to the little girl, *"Talitha, cumi,"* which is translated, *Little girl, I say to you, arise.* Immediately, the girl arose and walked.

Whatever you need from God it is in your tongue. Speak It!

God's Promise for You Today
(Meditate)

Proverbs 18:21 (KJV)

"Death and life are in the power of the tongue: and they that love it shall eat the fruit thereof."

Acts 17:28 (KJV)

"For in him we live, and move, and have our being."

Mark 11:23-25 (NKJV)

"For assuredly, I say to you, whoever says to this mountain, Be removed and be cast into the sea, and does not doubt in his heart, but believes that those things he says will be done, he will have whatever he says."

Journal Your Journey

Consider yourself, family, friends, and circumstances, what are the areas that appear to be sleep? Use your power and speak life over these areas today. Write out your declaration.

Day 6
Death and Life is in The Tongue Speak It!

_____

_____

_____

_____

_____

_____

_____

_____

_____

_____

_____

_____

_____

_____

_____

_____

_____

_____

_____

_____

_____

_____

_____

_____

_____

_____

_____

_____

_____

_____

_____

_____

_____

_____

_____

_____

_____

_____

_____

The power of your

words will declare

Your Destiny!

~Dr. Bendetta Perry

Day 7

I Declare!

I Declare:

I am... **Strong!**

I am... **Victorious!**

I am... **Calm!**

I am... **Content!**

I am... **Secure!**

I am... **Fortified!**

I am... **Fruitful!**

I am... **Progressive!**

I am... **Ingenious!**

I am... **Powerful!**

I am... **Fabulous!**

I am...**Expecting God's Goodness to unfold over me daily!**

<u>God's Promise for You Today</u>
(Meditate)

Proverbs 18:21 (NIV)

"Death and life are in the power of the tongue and they that love it shall eat the fruit thereof."

Proverbs 15:4 (NLT)

"Gentle words are a tree of life; a deceitful tongue crushes the spirit."

Ephesians 4:25 (NIV)

"Therefore each of you must put off falsehood and speak truthfully to your neighbor, for we are all members of one body."

Journal Your Journey

Write out a list of your declarations. You can use the "I am..." statements you have just read or create new ones. Expand on the "I am..." statement with an example of how you are walking in that declarations today.

Day 7
I Declare!

_____

_____

_____

_____

_____

_____

_____

_____

_____

_____

_____

_____

_____

_____

_____

_____

_____

_____

_____

_____

_____

_____

_____

Friends come and go, but a friend in Jesus is for Life! Right there in all times!

~Dr. Bendetta Perry

Day 8

Have You Met My Friends?

wo close friends came by to visit early this morning. I was awakened by a gentle knock on the door of my heart. I said within my spirit, "Who is there?"

It was Mercy and Goodness who stop by to embrace me with their presence. I had met them both long ago as a teenager in the 1970's. They wanted me to know they had never left me in all those years since our first encounter.

I will never forget the night I met Mercy and Goodness. It was a hot summers night, and I had just left a youth service at the church I attended. I was thirsty and walked to the corner store to buy a soda before walking home, which was only about 10 minutes away. After leaving the store I attempted to cross a street with no crosswalk or traffic light to get home. As I stepped off the curb, I heard the voice of the angel Mercy whispering in my ear, "Step back, you left your bible on the counter of the store."

I immediately took one step back without turning around, and there came a car speeding so fast, that if I had not step back, the impact of the car would have left me badly wounded or dead. The driver saw me and tried to put on breaks, but he couldn't break fast enough because of the high speed. All anyone could hear was the screeching of tires going through the intersection, which left tire marks on the pavement of the streets. Patrons of local businesses poured unto the sidewalks to see who had been hit.

The angel Goodness surround me that night, as I stood in amazement that God had just spared my life right before my eyes. If you ever have the chance to meet my friends, Mercy and Goodness, remember to do your part, *Listen and Obey*.

God's Promise for You Today
(Meditate)

Psalm 91:9-15 (NIV)

If you say, "The Lord is my refuge," and you make the Most High your dwelling. No harm will overtake you, no disaster will come near your tent. For he will command his angels concerning you to guard you in all your ways. They will lift you up in their hands, so that you will not strike your foot against a stone. You will tread on the lion and the cobra; you will trample the great lion and the serpent. Because he loves me, "says the Lord, "I will rescue him; for he acknowledges my name. He will call on me, and I will answer him; I will be with him in trouble, I will deliver him and honor him. With long life I will satisfy him and show him my salvation.

2 Thessalonians 3:3 (NIV)

"But the Lord is faithful, and he will strengthen you and protect you from the evil one."

Psalm 46:1(NIV)

"God is our refuge and strength, an ever-present help in trouble."

Journal Your Journey

Are you an acquaintance of Goodness and Mercy? Explain a time in your life when Goodness and Mercy were with you when you least expected their company.

_____

_____

_____

_____

_____

_____

_____

_____

_____

_____

_____

_____

_____

_____

_____

_____

_____

_____

_____

_____

_____

_____

_____

_____

_____

Day 8
Have You Met My Friends?

Guard the gate of your mind. It is not a playground for every negative thought to enter therein!

~ Dr. Bendetta Perry

Day 9

Shut the Gate!

*T*oo often, we leave our minds open to receive negative words which attack our thought life. We become open prey for the enemy to distract us from our God given purpose and keep us from destiny. I call that, *playing with the devil.*

The devil does not like you, and he is not playing with you. His total reason for existence is to kill, steal, and destroy you. He is not your friend and he does not fight fair.

Gates are design to protect you and keep unwanted visitors out and off your property. You belong to the Lord and He is commanding you to keep the gate shut; the gate of your mind, where the enemy comes in to attack your thought life with untruth, seductive spirits, deception, false witness, lies, adultery, fornication, uncleanness, lustful, idolatry, witchcraft, hatred, fits of rage, selfish ambition, dissentions, envy, and drunkenness; these are the works of the flesh set up like traps to keep you captive.

When the gate of your mind is left open, it's like a broad gate leading to destruction; many negative thoughts have access to enter through it, which can cause you to become spiritually dead.

To keep the gate of your mind closed from sinful thoughts that can bring you down, you must feed your spirit with thoughts that are honest, pure, noble, right, lovely, and of good report.

Become a student of the Word of God, for it will be a shield around you and direct your steps in the right path. A righteous man falls seven times and rises again, but the wicked stumble and calamity strikes. There is a battle for the mind; we have to prepare for the battle and learn how to take the enemy down, which is the strong hold that attack our minds and does not want to let go. The scriptures enlighten us to truth:

2 Corinthians10:4 *"For the weapons of our warfare are not carnal, but mighty through God to the pulling down of strong holds." Shut the gate of your mind and begin to sing praise songs and worship the Lord in spirit and truth. Praise is a powerful weapon against the enemy. Speak God's word over your life. Use your weapon of warfare and live with a victoriously life in Christ.*

God's Promise for You Today
(Meditate)

Psalm 118:19 (NIV)

"Open to me the gates of righteousness, I shall enter through them, I shall give thanks to the Lord."

Matthew 7:13 (NIV)

"Enter through the narrow gate, for the gate is wide and the way is broad that leads to destruction, and there are many who enter through it."

Romans 12:2 (ASV)

"Be not conformed to this world but be transferred by the renewing of your mind, so that you may prove what the will of God is, that which is good acceptable and perfect."

Journal Your Journey

Now that you are more aware of what strongholds have access to the different gates in your mind, which gates do you believe have been left open? Identify those gates and strongholds, and write a prayer to God, confessing the error and sealing those gates with the blood of Jesus.

_____

_____

_____

_____

_____

_____

_____

_____

_____

_____

_____

_____

_____

_____

_____

_____

_____

_____

_____

_____

_____

_____

_____

_____

_____

_____

_____

_____

_____

_____

_____

_____

_____

_____

_____

_____

_____

_____

_____

_____

_____

Kingdom

steppers never step

backwards.

Keep stepping

Forward!

~ Dr. Bendetta Perry

Day 10

Kingdom Access

od has given His body of believers Kingdom Access. "Kingdom" in the Greek is pronounced *basileia,* it means royal power, kingship, dominion, rule, and reign. It's the royal power and authority conferred on the body of believers in the Messiah's Kingdom.

The word "Access" means the ability to enter in. As royal citizens of the Kingdom of God, you have access given to you to enter territory in an area of land under the jurisdiction of a state or region, which is any place that is distinct from another area.

You are God's Ambassadors. He has given you authority in the realm of the spirit through prayer and the reading of His word, to know who you are and take the Keys of the Kingdom, to bind anything not lining up with His word, and to lose the blessing and righteousness of God.

The power of death and life are in your tongue, and those who love it will eat its fruit. As Ambassadors, you must learn to call those things that are not, as though they are. A passport will only take you so far, but *Kingdom Access* will take you to every place that the sole of your feet shall tread for God's Kingdom.

In 2009 I embarked a missionary journey with the Christian Women Devotional Alliance/Women of Strength Courage and Diversity. Nineteen women of faith traveled to another country, and we all needed passports to enter in.

As we walked through customs to get our luggage, two other ladies and I were pulled out of line and each question individually; what was our purpose for coming to their country, how long will you be staying, and our occupation?

It did not matter to customs that I had a passport. They wanted the questions answered and to their liking. In that moment, *Kingdom Access* was greater than my passport. We were able to tell customs that we had been given permission from the fourth largest mall in the world, which was located in their country, to give a gospel concert and to share a smile to everyone we met, and that everything had been set up months ahead of time through the mission leader.

Immediately after 25 minutes of being questioned, we were told permission was granted to enter their country. God had granted permission in the heavenly realm for our mission group to tread over this territory and region for His Glory. We stayed in that region 4 days and passed out 6,000 bible tracts telling of God's plan of salvation.

Today is your day to say yes to the assignment of God on your life.

God's Promise for You Today
(Meditate)

Ephesians 2:10 (ESV)

"For we are his workmanship, created in Christ Jesus for good works, which God prepared beforehand, that we should walk in them."

Jeremiah 29:11 (NIV)

"For I know the plans I have for you, declares the LORD, plans to prosper you and not to harm you, plans to give you hope and a future."

Romans 8:28 (KJV)

"And we know that all things work together for good to them that love God, to them who are the called according to his purpose."

Journal Your Journey

Write about your Kingdom Access. What doors has God given you access to open? Have you began exercising your authority by walking in your assignment?

_____

_____

_____

_____

_____

_____

_____

_____

_____

_____

_____

_____

_____

_____

_____

_____

_____

_____

_____

Answered prayer has no expiration date!

~ Dr. Bendetta Perry

Day 11

Woman with the Issue of Blood

The Woman Who Was Healed by a Touch
Matthew 9:20-22; Mark 5:25-34; Luke 8:43-48

An ailing unnamed woman was set free, after a hemorrhage lasting for twelve years, approximately 4,380 long days of her life, where she was rendered legally unclean according to the Levitical Law, Leviticus 15:19.

She could not throw herself at the feet of Christ and state her complaint without being stoned for being seen in public. Her fear, uncleanness, and pressure of the crowd made close contact with Jesus (Yeshua) nearly impossible; hence her fervor to touch, in some unnoticeable way, the tassels of His tallit (hem of His garment).

Who was this woman of great faith? Romans 10:17 *"For faith comes by hearing, and hearing by the word of God."* This woman had to have known the Old Testament Law.

Numbers 15:38-39 speaks to the children of Israel, and says to them, *"They shall make for themselves fringes on the corners of their garments... And this shall be tzitzit for you, and when you see it, you will remember all the commandments of God and perform them."*

Malachi 4:2 *"But unto you that fear my name shall the Sun of righteousness arise with healing in his wings."*

She was cured after years of humiliation, shame, and disappointment.

What this ailing woman really endured at the hands of the doctors in her era, is left to the imagination. A touch of reality is given to her story by the knowledge that she had suffered many things by many physicians, and was no better, but rather *grew worse.*

Where physicians failed, Christ succeeded. The woman with the issue of blood had to believe God for a miracle. She knew that she needed to be made whole of the everyday loss of blood that was making her weaker by the day. This woman undoubtedly heard of Jesus' power through God to heal.

Luke 5:31 Jesus stated, *"They that are whole have no need of a physician, but they that are sick."* Matthew 4:23 *"Jesus went throughout Galilee, teaching in their synagogues, proclaiming the good news of the kingdom, and healing every disease and sickness among the people."*

The lame walk, blind see, deaf hear, mute talk, and the dead are raised alive again. For she said, *"If I may touch but his clothes (hem of his garment) I shall be made whole. And straightway the fountain of her blood was dried up, and she felt in her body that she was healed of that plague." Mark 5:28-29*

She learned to trust God with her issue.

Issues, we all have issues that seem to overwhelm us with the fear of never being set free. What is your issue? A bad relationship, unemployment, transportation, an employer who over looks your promotion, unfaithful spouse, loss of a love one, disobedient children, a house that has been in escrow too long, and so forth. Like the Woman with the Issue of Blood, take your issue to God by faith, touch the hem of Yeshua's garment and be made whole.

The Woman with the Issue of Blood took a bold step of faith. Take that step of faith today and be set free of your *issue*. God's throne and healing power awaits you. Embrace His presence today and always.

God's Promise for You Today
(Meditate)

Hebrews 11:6 (KJV)

"But without faith is impossible to please him: for he that comes to God must believe that he is, and he is a rewarded of them that diligently seek him."

Hebrews 4:15-16 (NKJV)

"For we do not have a High Priest who cannot sympathize with our weaknesses, but was in all points tempted as we are, yet without sin. Let us therefore come boldly to the throne of God's grace, that we may obtain mercy and find grace to help in time of need."

Psalm 103:2-3(NIV)

"Praise the Lord, my Soul, and forget not all his benefits, who forgives all your sins and heals all your diseases."

Journal Your Journey

---

*What is your issue? Have you been living
with something that has been draining
life from you? Journal the issue and
faithfully see yourself touching Jesus.
It is time to be made whole.*

Day 11
The Women with the Issue of Blood

God heals broken hearts. Give him all the pieces!

~ Dr. Bendetta Perry

Day 12

Unbreak My Heart

*H*ave you ever had your heart broken? It's a pain that, for a moment in time, seems like it will last forever. It is typically caused by the death of a loved one, situations that you believed were secure on your job, home, finances, disobedience of a child, or the ending of a romantic relationship.

Hurt, disappointments, and pain can leave us all vulnerable and in need of support and a listening ear. Our pain isn't hidden from God. He offers us a healing oasis where we receive unconditional love, poured out on us from our Heavenly Father.

When God looks at us, even in our exposed state, He doesn't see us covered in shame. Instead, He is a loving God who is knocking at the door of your heart to comfort, restore, and heal you, emotionally and physically. God does not want you to have anxiety, but to cast all your cares on Him, because He cares for you. God is not like man with a broken and contrite heart. God will not despise. He will not leave you broken.

Our God will restore what is broke and change it into something amazing, all you need is faith. Your weeping may endure for a night, but there is the promise of joy in the morning.

Still hurting? Embrace the loving arms of Christ Jesus and receive the peace of God that passes all understanding.

<u>God's Promise for You Today</u>
(Meditate)

Psalm 34:18 (NIV)

"The Lord is near to those that have a broken heart, and save such as have a contrite spirit."

Psalm 73:26 (NIV)

"My flesh and my heart fail; but God is the strength of my heart and my portion forever."

Joel 2:25 (KJV)

"I will repay you for the years the locusts have eaten, the cankerworm, and the caterpillar, and the palmerworm, my great arm which I sent among you."

Journal Your Journey

Have you given God all the broken pieces of your heart? How has God turned your broken pieces into promises of Joy?

Day 12
Unbreak My Heart

_____

_____

_____

_____

_____

_____

_____

_____

_____

_____

_____

_____

_____

_____

_____

_____

_____

_____

_____

*Love sees no color
and speaks every
Language!*

~ Dr. Bendetta Perry

Day 13

Love Inspiration

*L*adies! Gentlemen! It's Valentine's Day! It's flower day! It's candy day! It's the heartfelt and romantic card day! Did you know that an estimated $18 billion dollars will be spent to show how much love means to so many people?

February 14th will be a very happy day for so many. Many will give and receive gifts that express love and admiration, but many more will not? So many hearts will swell with appreciation and worth, while so many more hearts will shrivel into heart break and low self-esteem.

A great songstress made these words famous, "What's love got to do with it?" Love and hate are the most powerful emotions that a person can express towards another. On this especial man-made day, *love* has everything to do with it.

For God is love, and it is only the love of God in a person that can truly love you the way you deserve to be loved. Who doesn't want to be loved? Everyone is looking for love, and on that one day of the year, that's considered to be that special day of love, so many are sadly affected.

How do I survive that day, or every day, and feel good about myself, if another human being doesn't express to me how special I am to them? There's a scripture in the Bible that tells us to love one another. It tells us to *love*.

Love is an action word followed by kindness, which comes straight from the heart without game or motive. Be that special someone that gives love to others. If you wait for someone to love you, you might be waiting for a while. But if you give love, love is immediate. If you hug someone, a hug in return is immediately given. Inspire others to love by loving others. Love one another.

God's Promise for You Today
(Meditate)

1 Corinthians 13:1-3 (NIV)

"Love is patient, love is kind. It does not envy. It does not boast, it is not proud. It does not dishonor others, it is not self-seeking, it is not easily angered, it keeps no record of wrongs. Love does not delight in evil but rejoices with the truth. It always protects, always trusts, always hopes, always perseveres. Love never fails.

Ephesians 4:2-3 (NIV)

"Be completely humble and gentle, be patient, bearing with one another in love. Make every effort to keep the unity of the spirit through the bond of peace.

1 Peter 4:8 (NIV)

"Above all, love each other deeply, because love covers a multitude of sins."

Journal Your Journey

Be a Love Inspiration. Write a Love letter to someone in your life, perhaps, family, friend, or acquaintance, and express your appreciation for who they are.

You are

God's Designer

Original Fragrance,

created for His purpose to

release His sweet-smelling

aroma to the world!

~ Dr. Bendetta Perry

Day 14

The Cost of Your Perfume

we, what is the cost of your perfume?

In order to release a sweet-smelling aroma in the lives of others, and in the sight of God, you have to be broken in spirit and allow God to cleanse your heart of everything that is not like Him.

In the book of Luke, a woman who was known as a sinner entered the house of a Pharisee where Jesus was reclining. She broke her alabaster box of perfume, that was worth a year's wages, to anoint Christ feet for her sins, which were many and was forgiven as she wept vehemently at His feet. Washing His feet with her tears, she wiped them with the hair on her head, and kissed Christ's feet to anointed them with the fragrant oil.

It cost her a great value to worship and give God thanks for all the love He showed her, by forgiving her sin and debt, and setting her free of the demons that tormented her and wanted to keep her bound in darkness.

The Pharisee's of that day did not think she was good enough to be in their presence and could not understand why Jesus would talk to such a woman. Jesus boldly spoke up for the woman by addressing to Simeon, *"Do you see this woman? I entered your house; you gave me no water for my feet, but she has washed my feet with her tears and wiped them with the hair of her head, kiss my feet since the time I enter into your house, and anointed my head with fragrant oil and you have not done any of things that she did for me and I was your guest. Her sins which are many are forgiven for she loved much."*

It does not matter what you've been through or what has happened to you. Like the woman that was a known sinner in her era, leave your hurt at the feet of Jesus and release the sweet aroma of Christ that is within you, to the world.

2 Corinthians 2:14-`5 *"Now thanks be to God, who in Christ always leads us in triumphal procession, and through us spreads the fragrance of the knowledge of him everywhere. For we are the aroma of Christ to God among those who are being saved and among those who are perishing."*

God loves you so much more than what you could ever imagine.

God's Promise for You Today
(Meditate)

Ephesians 5:1-2 (ESV)

"Therefore, be imitators of God as beloved children, and walk in love, just as Christ also loved you and gave himself up for us, a fragrant offering and a sacrifice to God."

Philippians 4:18 (NIV)

"I have received full payment and have and have more than enough. I am amply supplied, having received from Epaphroditus the gifts you sent. They are a fragrant offering, an acceptable sacrifice, well-pleasing to God."

Isaiah 1:18 (NIV)

"Come now, let us settle the matter," says the Lord. "though your sins are like scarlet, they shall be as white as snow, though they are red as crimson, they shall be like wool, sins."

Journal Your Journey

Journal your alabaster experience.
What have you laid before Jesus to expose
your sweet-smelling perfume?

Day 14
The Cost of Your Perfume

Day 14
The Cost of Your Perfume

_____

_____

_____

_____

_____

_____

_____

_____

_____

_____

_____

_____

_____

_____

_____

_____

_____

_____

_____

_____

_____

_____

Come, what may.

I will be Victorious!

I will not be Defeated!

~ Dr. Bendetta Perry

Day 15

Overcoming Defeat

 $\mathcal{M}$ any times in my life, I have felt defeated. Not only did I feel defeated, I was defeated. The spirit of depression was trying to overtake me. I prayed to the Lord and He reminded me of a familiar scripture in the bible.

1 Corinthians 15:57, *"But thanks be to God, who gives us the victory through our Lord Jesus Christ."*

God's love gave me the confidence that I needed to move from defeat, to wholeness of mind.

My Plan of Action to Move Forward

1. Getting up and pressing forward towards my dream.
2. Wiping my tears and placing a smile on my face.
3. Realizing that the final chapter of my life has not been written.
4. Acknowledging that I hold the pen that writes my destiny.

With a positive mindset, I declared the truth of God's word in my life. I am not alone. God will never leave me nor forsake me in any situation.

Romans 8:37, *"In all these things we are more than conquerors through him who loved us."*

I embraced God's ultimate plan for my life, and everyone who hopes in him must take that step of faith to trust His will for their life.

Today I stand Victorious! No longer the Victim of Defeat.

God's Promise for You Today
(Meditate)

Jeremiah 29:11(NIV)

"For I know the plans I have for you,' declares the LORD, 'plans to prosper you and not to harm you, plans to give you hope and a future."

Joshua 1:9 (NIV)

"Be Strong and Courageous. Do not be afraid, do not be discouraged. For the Lord your God will be with you wherever you go."

1 John 5:4 (NIV)

"For everyone who has been born of God overcomes the world. And this is the victory that has overcome the world even our faith."

Journal Your Journey

What is your plan of action to overcome defeat? Write out your strategy and your go to scriptures to help you strive towards God plan for your life.

_____

_____

_____

_____

_____

_____

_____

_____

_____

_____

_____

_____

_____

_____

_____

_____

_____

_____

_____

_____

_____

_____

_____

Day 15
Overcoming Defeat

A creative

mind has

No Boarders.

~ Dr. Bendetta Perry

Day 16

Be Prolific

here is a word that God spoke in my spirit early one morning, the word was "Prolific." I had never heard the word before and immediately I wanted to know the meaning. I embraced it with enthusiasm, excitement, and honor that God would reveal *prolific* to me. It means productive, creative, inventive, bringing forth much fruit in every area of our lives (large amount of quality).

"Hallelujah, Glory to God," are the words that flowed out of my mouth and spirit. There was an immediate impact on me; change has to be made.

God is calling us to: "Be Prolific."

The first step in being prolific is to stay connected to God. Jesus said: *"I am the vine you are the branches. If you remain in me and I in you, you will bring forth much fruit, apart from me you can do nothing." John 15:5*

The second step is to know your calling. What has God called you to do for His Kingdom? God will give you passion to complete the assignment He has placed on your life, as you go forth in your gifting.

Third, you must remain steadfast and not allow yourself to be distracted from your goal by every disturbance sent to keep you from pursing your purpose, which is the reason why God created you. Fourth, you must study the assignment God has given you and all that comes with becoming a person of excellence, to show yourself approve unto God, a vessel that will not bring shame, but bring Glory to the Lord.

Fifth, you must embrace the new horizon of where God is taking you and the people He will connect to you, as you go forward to reign in destiny and territory, fearlessly knowing God is with you, and His Spirit lives within you.

And the final step six, see yourself victorious and the battle is already won, for you walk by overcoming faith and you are more than a conqueror in Christ Jesus.

God's Promise for You Today
(Meditate)

Genesis 39:2 (NIV)

"The Lord was with Joseph so he prospered, and he lived in the house of his Egyptian mastered."

Psalm 1:1-3 (NIV)

"Blessed is the one who does not walk in the step with the wicked or stand in the way that sinners take or sit in the company of mockers, but his delight is in the law of the Lord, and who meditates on his law day and night. That person is like a tree planted by streams of water, which yields its fruit in season and whose leaf does not wither and whatever they do prospers."

Proverbs 16:3 9 (NIV)

"Commit to the Lord whatever you do, and he will establish your plans."

Journal Your Journey

Review the steps of being prolific and determine if you are currently walking in these steps. Write out a plan of how you will walk out each action step and refer to it daily.

Day 16
Be Prolific

Joy is like a running river within the soul that is far greater than momentary happiness.

~ Dr. Bendetta Perry

Day 17

Today I Chose JOY!

e joyful. Today I chose Joy. Joy is greater than happiness. Joy comes from the Holy Spirit abiding within you and is based on a relationship with God that is forgiving and real. Joy is within the heart of a person and is release in the atmosphere of others whom they connect with, and joy will always bring a pleasant aroma.

There is joy in heaven over an unbeliever's conversion to accept Christ. The Lord, Himself, told us to rejoice that our names are written in heaven.

Joy comes through wisdom of understanding the true meaning of life and having contentment and peace of mind over issues that would otherwise disturb your happiness. You can rejoice because of the truth, "All things work together for the good to them that love the Lord and are called for His purpose."

Do you truly understand God's call on your life? It is the reason why you exist. Think about it for a moment, knowing this will bring about a God given passion to fulfill your destiny, which is real Joy. Your calling brings Joy which is far greater than happiness.

Happiness is based on temporary circumstances, job, people, money, love relationships, and promises which are all subject to change at any given moment, and when all that you hope for is gone, there is no more happiness or foundation to stand on.

Joy is one of the Fruits of the Spirit, the character of God, that dwells within you when you accept His plan of salvation, through His son, and invite the Holy Spirit to dwell within you.

God's Promise for You Today
(Meditate)

Proverbs 17:22 (ESV)

"A joyful heart is good medicine, but a crushed spirit dries up the bones."

Psalm 16:11 (NASB)

"You will make known to me the path of life; in your presence is fullness of joy; in your right hand there are pleasures forever."

Romans 15:13 (NIV)

"May the God of hope fill you with all joy and peace as you trust in him, so that you may overflow with hope by the power of the Holy Spirit."

Journal Your Journey

Have you been mistaking happiness for joy? List the people or things in your life that you depend on and consider if these things are a foundation for temporary happiness or permanent Joy? How do they support the plan and purpose for your life?

God's Word is a
mirror reflecting your
beauty and smile.
Stay in the mirror of
God's Word!

~ Dr. Bendetta Perry

Day 18

A Smile is Powerful

A smile is always attractive and embracing like the sweet-smelling aroma of perfume. It uplifts the atmosphere in a room by releasing kindness, acceptance, confidence, joy, and laughter in the lives of the people embracing its fragrance.

A smile invites the other person to smile back, and allows the world to know that the best things in life are free; such as: the laughter of children playing, time spent with family, the company of true friends, a carefree walk, a refreshing jog, bike riding, swimming, the smell of the ocean, the breath taking sight of the mountains, beautiful flowers, the aroma of fresh green grass, a song of praise, the love of God, and hope of a prosperous future.

A smile is powerful. It brings healing to those who have lost hope and gives the person who embraces the kindness of your smile, the assurance of knowing that someone cares. A sincere smile can turn an enemy to a friend, a person who has given up on life a reason to live on, it offers the person without a smile a reason to smile and turns someone's bad attitude into a sweet-smelling aroma.

As a child, I rarely smiled and was very sensitive. Classmates would tease me and call me, "Cry Baby," because I would be in tears at the drop of hat. One day we were having recess, and someone made fun of me, and I begin to cry. The teacher became so angry at me for crying, she decided to end recess early and everyone had to return to the classroom.

My classmates were so upset that their fun had been cut short. The last thing I felt like doing was smiling, and I was trying so hard to smile and not to cry. It was as if I was in a world that I did not fit into. Inwardly, I felt within myself that my happiness is connected to someone or something that I have not encountered at this season of my life.

At age 16, I received Christ as my savior and my whole life turned around. I experienced the joy of the Lord from being in His presence and it caused me to smile everywhere I went. I soon learned that there is a difference between joy and happiness. Happiness is for a moment and is based on temporary situations. Joy is based on the knowledge of knowing God, His unfailing love for you, and your relationship with him which causes you to sincerely smile as you encounter people daily and release His love to the world.

For those looking for happiness, God never promised you happiness, but He did promise you Joy. Bless someone's life today by releasing the aroma of your Smile. It impacts the lives of others.

God's Promise for You Today
(Meditate)

Proverbs 15:13-15 (NLT)

"A glad heart makes a cheerful face, but by sorrow of heart the spirit is crushed. The heart of him who has understanding seeks knowledge, but the mouths of fools feed on folly. All the days of the afflicted are evil, but the cheerful of heart has a continual feast."

Job 82:1 (NIV)

"He will yet fill your mouth with laughter and your lips with shouts of joy."

Psalm 16:11 (NIV)

"You make known to me the path of life: in your presence there is fullness of joy, at your right hand are pleasures forevermore."

Journal Your Journey

Practice your gift giving today and offer a smile to everyone you encounter. At the end of your day, journal your experiences and list all the gifts you received in return. How powerful was your smile?

_____

_____

_____

_____

_____

_____

_____

_____

_____

_____

_____

_____

_____

_____

_____

_____

_____

_____

_____

_____

_____

Day 18
A Smile is Powerful

The confident woman never has restraint in giving another woman a compliment, for she is never in competition with another woman.

~ Dr. Bendetta Perry

Day 19

The Confident Women

The Confident Woman demonstrates leadership, true beauty, and walks with God's favor upon her life. She is very aware of who she is; therefore, she respects herself and everyone who she comes in contact with and does not throw away her confidence, which will be richly rewarded.

The Confident Woman has no restraint in giving another woman a compliment, for she is never in competition with another woman. She encourages everyone, male or female, to become the best that God has called them to be and push towards their purpose and destiny.

The Confident Woman knows the giver of real love (*God*) and therefore, she has no problem with giving or receiving love. She is a virtuous woman and a crown to her husband.

The Confident Woman always speaks with words of wisdom and listens with a heart of genuine concern. She has learned one of the greatest gifts, that God has given to the human race, is to care for one another.

The Confident Woman wholeheartedly trusts in every word of the living God. She knows that God is not a man that He should lie to her. (*Numbers 23:19*)

The Confident Woman has learned many valuable lessons from her past. She handles her present with wisdom and with grace as she walks towards her future.

The Confident Woman is a First-Class Lady.

God's Promise for You Today
(Meditate)

Philippians 1:6 (NIV)
"Being confident of this, that he who began a good work in you will carry it on to completion until the day of Christ Jesus."

Isaiah 32:17 (NIV)
"The fruit of that righteousness will be peace, its effect will be quietness and confidence forever."

Ephesians 3:12 (NIV)
"In him and through faith in him we may approach God with freedom and confidence."

Journal Your Journey

Create your own passage of The Confident Women. Who are you as a confident woman, or who is it that you will become?

_____

_____

_____

_____

_____

_____

_____

_____

_____

_____

_____

_____

_____

_____

_____

_____

_____

The confident man does not have to love a thousand women. He just needs to love one woman in a thousand ways. And she will love him back in a thousand ways!

~ Dr. Bendetta Perry

Day 20

I Finally Met Him!

I finally met him!

You know that man that my mother and her friends always talked about? I used to hear my mother and her friends say, "There is nothing better than being in a relationship with a *Confident Man.*"

They would say that a *Confident Man* does not have to love a thousand women; he only has to love one woman in a thousand ways, and in return she loves him back in a thousand ways.

I was just a young girl of about 12 years old, and I know that I should have never listen to their conversation, but I could not wait to grow up and meet me a *Confident Man.*

Well, I grew up and met many men, but none of them fit the description of that man my mother and her friends would talk about.

After many years of dating and discouragement, I finally gave up on ever meeting the *Confident Man*.

One day I was home, reading my bible and praying, and a light from heaven begin to shine in my spirit as I read Jeremiah 29:11, *"I know the plans I have for you, declares the Lord, plans to prosper you and not to harm you plans to give you hope and a future."*

For the first time I realize that God had a wonderful plan for my life and that He loves me. At that point I begin to walk in God's purpose for my life and reign in the destiny that He called me to, as a kingdom citizen and believer of all God's promises to me.

As I was walking in God's assignment for my life, he saw me, the *Confident Man*, the one my mother and her friends talked about, and he loved God with all his heart. I finally met him! I guess there was one thing my mother and her friends forgot to mention in their conversation,

In order to meet the *Confident Man,*
you need to be the *Confident Woman.*

God's Promise for You Today
(Meditate)

Hebrews 10:35-36 (ESV)

"Therefore do not throw away your confidence, which has a great reward. For you have need of endurance, so that when you have done the will of God you may receive what is promised."

Psalm 27:3 (ESV)

"Though an arm encamp against me, my heart shall not fear; though war arise against me, yet I will be confident."

Psalm 138:8 (ESV)

"The Lord will fulfill his purpose for me your steadfast love, O Lord, endures forever. Do not forsake the work of your hands."

Journal Your Journey

---

*Have you met the confident man?
If not, what areas in your life need to be
strengthened with the knowledge of God?
As you confidently trust God to
strengthen every area of your life, you
also give Him permission to divinely send
the Confident Man directly to you.*

_____

_____

_____

_____

_____

_____

_____

_____

_____

_____

_____

_____

_____

_____

_____

_____

_____

_____

_____

_____

Day 20
I Finally Met Him!

Love is an action word followed by kindness. Kindness is a gentle behavior towards another person that comes from the heart without game or motive. God's love is full of action and kindness!

~ Dr. Bendetta Perry

Day 21

God is Not a Silent Lover

God is not a silent lover. He has declared His love for you before the world. A lover is a person who greatly enjoys your presence and has great affection towards you. A lover understands that love is an action word followed by acts of kindness, without game or motive towards the recipient of love.

The day God gave His only begotten Son, *that whosoever believes in Him would not perish but have eternal life*, was the day that all those whom believed became a recipient of love.

God's love is like the morning dew, always refreshing, restoring, and reliable. When all fails you can depend on God and His word. *"Be strong and courageous the Lord will go before you. He will be with you, he will not leave you or forsake you,"* *Deuteronomy 31:6.*

God is passionate about His own love for us and is always demonstrating the power of His unconditional love daily. While we were doing our own thing, getting high, swearing, lying, full of hatred, adultery, murder, and so forth, Christ died for us. Christ victory on the cross, over death and the grave, has brought us into an intimate love relationship with God that is real and personal.

Once you experience the love of God, your heart should be directed towards Him to do the things that please Him. Apostle Paul prayed for the Thessalonian church in 2 Thessalonians 5:22, *"May the Lord direct your hearts into the love of God."* When the Lord takes a hold of the heart of His people and directs them into the love of God, they experience the outpouring of the His love through the Holy Spirit.

See what great love the Father has lavished on us, that we should be called children of God? And that is what we are! How sweet it is to be loved by God. God's love is sweeter than the honey in the honeycomb.

As we embrace His amazing love for us, morning by morning, new mercies we see, because His compassions fail not. We love Him because He first loved us.

There is no greater love than the love of God. For it is only the love of God in a person that can love you the way you deserve to be loved.

God is not a Silent Lover!

<u>God's Promise for You Today</u>
(Meditate)

Psalm 86:5 (NIV)

"You, Lord, are forgiving and good abounding in love to all who call to you."

Psalm 136:26 (NIV)

"Give thanks to the God of heaven, for his steadfast love endures forever."

Ephesians 2:4-5 (NIV)

"But God, being rich in mercy, because of the great love with which he loved us, even when we were dead in our trespasses, made us alive together with Christ – by grace you have been saved."

Journal Your Journey

Mirror the love of God and don't be a silent lover. Write your love letter to God. Acknowledge His love for you and let God know He has a hold of your heart.

_____

_____

_____

_____

_____

_____

_____

_____

_____

_____

_____

_____

_____

_____

_____

_____

_____

_____

Water, cooling, restoring, reviving, refreshing to the soul and body. Spiritual and natural water got to have it; can't live life without it. Water, God's gift to us. Enjoy!

~ Dr. Bendetta Perry

Day 22

Two Women at the Well

*L*ife can sometimes seem like a long journey, traveling across a dry desert, surrounded by unknown land, knowing that if you do not find water soon, your journey will result in great peril, distress, dehydration, or even death if there is no water to drink.

Have you ever found yourself in a dry place and thirsty for more than your present situation? Today I am reminded of a woman name Hagar. She was the maidservant of Sarah, the wife of the great patriarch Abraham.

Sarah gave Hagar to Abraham to bear a child, because she was barren and had no children, so the maidservant bore Abraham a son named Ishmael. God opened Sarah's womb and fulfilled His promise and she had a son named Isaac.

Sarah caught Ishmael mocking her son and she order Abraham to cast Hagar and Ishmael out of their camp. With bread and a skin of water, she was told to leave. Hagar and her son ended up in the desert and found themselves in a dry place with no water, for the water in the skin was used up. Hagar wept and cried out not to see her son die. Then God open her eyes and she saw a well of water. They survived the desert that was meant to destroy them.

You may be in a desert situation, but God is about to bring you out of all your dry places. Learn to believe God for all His promises to you. Trust God at His word. Isaiah 43:19, *"Behold, I will do a new thing; now it shall spring forth shall you not know it? I will even make a way in the wilderness, and rivers in the desert."*

There is another woman that had a *well* experience, she was known as the Samaritan Woman. She was thirsty in her soul for something greater than another dry relationship that left her empty and with a void of understanding, always looking for someone to satisfy her needs and quench the thirst within her.

This woman of Samaria went in the middle of the hot afternoon to draw water from Jacob's well, which was not the custom of Middle Eastern women; they filled their water jars in the early morning while it was cool. It is thought that she went in the afternoon to avoid the other women who shunned her, due to the reputation that she had with men.

That hot afternoon, Jesus was sitting on Jacob's well waiting for her. He spoke to the soul of the woman and asked for a drink of water, through that conversation the knowledge of Jesus being the Messiah was revealed to her. She begged Christ to give her the living water that she would never thirst again.

She confessed her sins of having five husbands by perceiving Christ was a prophet for knowing her life story. Being filled with the joy of the Lord, she left her water pot and ran to the city to invite the men to come meet a Man, who told of all things she ever did and that it could possibly be the Christ. This Samaritan woman became the first female Evangelist in Samaria.

Has life left you thirsty and searching for the things that cannot satisfy? Then ask Christ to fill you with His living water which comes with being filled with the Spirit of God. Beloved, God loves you today and always. He is right there with you in your desert, waiting to bring you out of all your dry places.

God's Promise for You Today
(Meditate)

Psalm 107:35 (ASV)

"He changes a wilderness into a pool of water and a dry land unto springs of water."

Isaiah 48:21 (ESV)

"They did not thirst when he led them through the deserts. He made the water flow out of the rock for them, He split the rock and the water gushed forth."

Isaiah 44:3 (NIV)

"For I will pour out water on the thirsty land and streams on the dry ground. I will pour out my spirit on your offspring and my blessing on your descendants."

Journal Your Journey

Jesus has met you at the
well today. He has come to saturate you
with His endless stream of water over
every dry place in your life. What are the
matters of your heart?

_____

_____

_____

_____

_____

_____

_____

_____

_____

_____

_____

_____

_____

_____

_____

_____

_____

_____

_____

_____

_____

_____

An unforgiving
heart will never
reach destiny,
Too Much
Blockage!

~ CHF

Day 23

Why Should I Forgive? They Hurt Me.

orgiveness sets the captive free, and the captive is you. The pain, anger, and roots of bitterness are memories of the past that can consume your mind, like a video camera playing over again in your head of yesterday hurt's. So many times, you want to stop the video, but the thoughts keep coming back and you feel powerless, unable to move forward with your life to pass the emotions that left you captive.

The Holy Spirit of God is right there with you. God wants to bring healing to your broken and wounded heart by creating in you a clean heart, renewing within you a right spirit, to be free of anguish, and exhale all of your pain at the altar of the Holy Spirit by embracing His presence of love, forgiveness, joy, gentleness, goodness, mercy, compassion, and complete healing in Him.

Forgiveness can come immediately, or it may be a process. Know this, the Holy Spirit is right there with you in the process. Forgiveness is the start of a new beginning and the vehicle that allows you to push forward. Unforgiveness causes you to have a collision, many never recover from it and are left paralyzed. Forgiveness does not excuse someone's behavior, but it releases you to experience peace that passes all understanding, and no one will ever be able to take that away from you again.

Chose forgiveness and move forward with your life. Forgiveness is like a sweet perfume. It changes the atmosphere of the person who is forgiven, allows them to be free, releases the person who forgave them, and to forgive others as Christ has forgiven them of their trespasses.

Release the aroma of forgiveness today and stay free.

God's Promise for You Today
(Meditate)

Colossians 3:13 (ESV)

"Bearing with one another and, if one has a complaint against another, forgiving each other, as the Lord has forgiven you, so you also must forgive."

Ephesians 4:31-32 (NIV)

"Get rid of all bitterness, rage and anger, brawling and slander, along with every form of malice." Be kind and compassionate to one another, forgiving each other just as in Christ God forgave you."

Matthew 6:14-15 (NIV)

Or if you forgive other people when they sin against you, your heavenly Father will also forgive you. For if you forgive other people when they sin against you, your heavenly Father will also forgive you.

Journal Your Journey

---

*Are you holding on to
unforgiveness in your heart?
Be free and release yourself from any
bondage of strife or unforgiveness. Walk
in the peace. If you are walking in the
Spirit of Peace, reflect on a time when you
had to forgive someone who may not have
deserved the forgiveness. What was the
process and how did the forgiveness
make you feel?*

_____

_____

_____

_____

_____

_____

_____

_____

_____

_____

_____

_____

_____

_____

_____

_____

_____

_____

_____

_____

_____

_____

_____

_____

_____

_____

_____

_____

_____

_____

_____

_____

_____

_____

_____

_____

_____

_____

Shift your

atmosphere from,

worry to Worship!

~ Dr. Bendetta Perry

Day 24

Worship and Praise, Defeat the Enemy

W orship is a lifestyle of adoration and reverence unto God, shown by your actions and response to everyday occurrences and situations that arise in our lives. Worship comes straight from the heart of your spirit and releases you to be free of anxiety, worry, fear, complaint, and ushers you to be amidst in His presence, that bring perfect peace.

God is a spirit and they that worship Him must worship Him in spirit and truth. The truth of reading God's word daily will cause you to reverence Him for the reality of who He is in your life, through prayer and the power to overcome the darts sent against you.

Praise is when we give God thanks for what He has already done for us. One of the words in the Hebrew for praise is "Hallah," which means to boast, brag, or rave about God even to the point of appearing foolish. Unfortunately, most of us are ashamed to shout, scream, and brag on God for fear that we may be labeled as fanatics.

Praise is a way of life for the upright in heart. Yadah, which is another Hebrew word for praise, means to extend hands in form of worship unto God. The bible tells us in Psalm 134:2, *"Lift up your hands in the sanctuary and praise the Lord."*

Today I encouraged you, no matter what you are facing at this very moment, lift up your hands and give God thanks and praise. The battle that you are facing is already won! King Jehosphaphat, the King of Judah, had a vast army coming up against him; all of Judah and Jerusalem from the territory of Ammon, Moab and Mount Seir.

Have you ever had so much pressure surrounding you that it felt like a vast army was arising against you? What did you do to overcome the situation?

King Jehosphaphat prayed and cried out to God, along with the people of Judah and Jerusalem. The Lord sent word, "The battle is not yours but the Lord," and to stand firm and as they went forth to battle. King Jehosphaphat appointed singers to lead the battle, praising God with a loud voice on high and singing, *"Praise the Lord, for his mercy endures forever."*

Immediately the Lord sent an ambush against the enemies of King Jehosphaphat, and all his enemies who were rising up against him, Judah, and Jerusalem, turned on one another and were all defeated and destroyed by their own hands.

I love to praise him. Praise defeats the enemy and gains you the Victory!

<u>God's Promise for You Today</u>
(Meditate)

Psalm 63:3-4 (NIV)

"Because your love is better than life, my lips will glorify you. I will praise you as long as I live, and in your name, I will lift up my hands."

Deuteronomy 10:21(NIV)

"He is the one you praise; he is your God, who performed for you those great and awesome wonders you saw with you own eyes."

Jeremiah 20:13 (NIV)

"Sing to the Lord, give praise to the Lord, He rescues the life of the needy from the hands of the wicked."

Journal Your Journey

Have you ever had so much pressure surrounding you that it felt like a vast army was arising against you? What did you do to overcome the situation?

Day 24
Worship and Praise Defeat the Enemy

_____
_____
_____
_____
_____
_____
_____
_____
_____
_____
_____
_____
_____
_____
_____
_____
_____
_____
_____
_____

_____

_____

_____

_____

_____

_____

_____

_____

_____

_____

_____

_____

_____

_____

_____

_____

_____

_____

_____

_____

_____

_____

God's love for you is infinite like the sand on the beach shore!

~ Dr. Bendetta Perry

Day 25

God's Incalculable Love for You

*H*ave you ever been in love and received a love letter from the one you love? One you kept for years and read over and over? One morning I woke up and read a love letter from God. I have read this letter many times in life. My heart was overwhelmed with love, as if it was the first time. The words of the letter captivated my heart in times past, today, and forever.

God's love letter to us is found in the Bible (*His Living Word*). His love letter breaths grace, forgiveness, hope, and righteousness through Christ. He speaks life over you every day through the reading of the scriptures because of His great love for you.

Let me ask you another question, have you ever thought about going to the beach and counting the grains of sand? Unthinkable to most of us, and a thought that never crossed our mind, other than playing in the sand, and building sandcastles.

According to an internet study, if you calculate how many grains of sand there are in a teaspoon, and then multiply it by all the beaches and desserts in the world, then the earth has roughly 7.5 x 1018 grains of sand or seven quintillion, five hundred quadrillion grains.

Did you know that God's love for you is greater in number than the sand, and that His love is immeasurable? The word of God states in Psalm 139:17-18, *"How great are your thoughts, about me, O God. They cannot be numbered! I can't even count them; they outnumber the grains of sand! And when I wake up, you are still with me."*

Lift your head and be encouraged today, for we are so loved by God. Our Heavenly Father lavishes His love upon us every day. His very thoughts are concerning you. Lavish is defined as regal, posh, splendid, and grand. This means all through the day, night, and when you awaken to the morning sun, God's heart, which is His thoughts, are still with you.

God's Love is perfect, steadfast, unequivocal, forgiving, all-inclusive, compassing, pure, lasting, sacrificially strong, enduring, refreshing, redeeming, everlasting, lavish, full, inspiring, hopeful, gracious, and so much more. It is never based on us, our abilities, or striving to ever be good enough. It's found in Him, His character, and a huge capacity to give. It knows no boundaries and has not limits. There is no place too deep that His love cannot reach.

Have you been searching for someone to love you sincerely and deeply? Greater love has no one than this; to lay down one's life for one's friends, and that is exactly what Christ did for you and me. God proved His own love for us in this. While we were yet doing our own thing and living without the knowledge of Christ in our hearts or minds, He sent His son to die for us and transferred us from the domain of darkness into the kingdom of His dear son.

The greatest love story that you will ever embrace is the one between you and Christ Jesus. God loves you so much more than you can imagine. You are God's letter to the world, releasing His sweet-smelling aroma in every place.

God's Promise for You Today
(Meditate)

1 John 4:7-11(NKJV)

"Beloved, let us love one another, for love is of God, and everyone who loves is born of God and knows God. He who does not love does not know God, for God is love. In this the love of God was manifested toward us. That God has sent His only begotten Son into the world, that we might live through Him. This is love, not that we loved God, but that He loved us and sent His Son to be the propitiation for our sins. Beloved, if God so loved us, we also ought to love one another."

1 John 3:1 (NIV)

"See what great love the Father has lavished on us, that we should be called children of God! And that is what we are."

Psalm 86:15 (KJV)

"But you, O Lord, are a compassionate and gracious God, slow to anger, abounding in love and faithfulness."

Journal Your Journey

Have you read your love letter from God? What does His word say about you? Be led by the Holy Spirit and write an actual love letter from God to you, using His Word.

_____

_____

_____

_____

_____

_____

_____

_____

_____

_____

_____

_____

_____

_____

_____

_____

_____

_____

_____

_____

_____

_____

The baton was

handed over to you.

Win!

~ Dr. Bendetta Perry

Day 26

Pick Up the Baton and Finish the Race

relay race is a track and field event, in which athletes run a preset distance carrying a baton before passing it to the next runner. In the relay, someone has been chosen to complete the race, which is the anchor leg. This person is the most experienced competitor on your team to receive the baton and run towards the finish line to complete the race. The anchor leg realizes the race is not given to the swift or the strong, but to one who endures unto the end (Ecclesiastes 9:11).

When the race is difficult, we like to blame circumstances or other people, and sometimes even God. The truth is you allowed yourself to become distracted. Distracted means unable to concentrate because one's mind is preoccupied, and you have lost sight of the goal.

In order to run effectively, the blood must flow properly to the heart and there cannot be any blockage. If we stumble or fall in the race of life, it is our own fault, because His divine power has given us all things that pertain to life and godliness. You are the one God has chosen to complete the race and to carry the baton of His word, which has been given to you through the testimonies of the biblical characters who have gone on before you, declaring God's word as truth.

The truth sets you free and gives you the ability to move forward towards your purpose and reign in your destiny, over the territory that God has called you to conquer for His glory, because of your steadfast, immoveable, always abounding in His will for your life.

God's Promise for You Today
(Meditate)

2 Timothy 4:7 (NIV)

"I have fought the good fight, I have finished the race, I have kept the faith."

1 Corinthians 9:24-27 (ESV)

"Do you not know that in a race all the runners run, but only one receives the prize? So run that you may obtain it. Every athlete exercises self-control in all things. They do it to receive a perishable wreath, but we an imperishable. So I do not run aimlessly; I do not box as one beating the air. But I discipline my body and keep it under control, lest after preaching to others I myself should be disqualified."

Psalm 18:29 (NIV)

"With your help I can advance against a troop, with my god I can scale on a wall."

Journal Your Journey

---

*God has chosen you to finish
the race. What has God trusted
in your hands to carry to the finish line?
Are there any blocks or distraction on the
track, preventing you from running
the race?*

_____

_____

_____

_____

_____

_____

_____

_____

_____

_____

_____

_____

_____

_____

_____

_____

_____

_____

_____

_____

Faith is the first action step to reach Success!

~ Dr. Bendetta Perry

Day 27

Action Done, Congratulations!

*F*aith is an action word that allows you to go forth into doing what God has called you to do. Faith moves the heart of God, and without faith you cannot please God. Faith is believing in God's word.

In Matthew 8:5-13, a Roman officer pleaded with Jesus to heal his servant, and the Lord responded, *"I will come and heal him."*

The officer said, *"Lord I am not worthy to have you come into my home. Just say the word from where you are, and my servant will be healed."*

When Jesus heard this, He was amazed. Turning to those who were following him, He said, *"I tell you the truth, I have not seen faith like that in all Israel."*

Here is a man that understood authority. The Roman officer's belief in Jesus' authority left him with no doubt, that his request for the healing of his servant would be granted without the need for the Lord Jesus to personally go to them.

Your faith is action and moves the heart of God. Does your faith in God allow you to believe that His word will do what it says? Awe, if it does not, then build your faith in the word of God, *for faith comes by hearing and hearing through the Word of God.*

Naaman was the great commander of Syria's army and was highly regarded for his many victories that God brought him. A valiant solider, but he had leprosy which was an incurable disease at that time. Naaman's wife had a young servant girl that had been captured from Israel and she told her mistress, *"If only my master would see the prophet who is in Samaria, he would cure him of his leprosy."*

Naaman receive permission from the King of Aram along with a letter to give to the King of Israel to cure him of his leprosy. The King tore his robes after reading the letter and said, *"Am I God?"*

When Elisha heard that the King tore his robes, he sent him a message, *"Why have you torn your robes? Have the man come to me and he will know that there is a prophet in Israel."*

Naaman, a great hero, was outraged when Elisha the prophet sent a messenger that said, *"Go wash yourself seven times in the Jordan, and your flesh will be restored, and you will be cleansed."* Namaan thought the Jordan River was dirty and beneath him to step into and be cleansed.

Naaman's servants advised him to take the word of the prophet and go wash in the Jordan and be cleansed. So, he went down and dipped himself in the Jordan seven times, as the man of God had told him, and his flesh was restored and became clean like that of a young boy.

Your faith is action and moves the heart and hand of God. Action done, Congratulations!

God's Promise for You Today
(Meditate)

Hebrews 11:1 (KJV)
"Now faith is the substance of things hoped for, the evidence of thing not seen."

Mark 11:24 (NIV)
"Therefore I tell you, whatever you ask for in prayer, believe that you have received it, and it will be yours.

Hebrews 11:16 (NIV)
"And without faith it is impossible to please God, because anyone who comes to him must believe that he exists and that he rewards those who earnestly seek him."

Journal Your Journey

How strong is your faith? What is it that God has told you to do? Write out what you are believing God for and search His Word for His answers and promises. Write out God's promises and put your faith in action by declare God's word over yourself, daily.

Day 27
Action Done, Congratulations!

_____

_____

_____

_____

_____

_____

_____

_____

_____

_____

_____

_____

_____

_____

_____

_____

_____

_____

Diamonds are rare and priceless. If you have a diamond in your life, treat that person special, because true friendships are priceless. Be a Diamond.

~ Dr. Bendetta Perry

Day 28

You Are God's Diamond for This World

*A*we! Beautiful, Glowing, Sparkling, Diamond. This is your season to shine like the stars in the universe. God has created you with purpose for the whole world to see. The word diamond comes from the Greek word "Adamas," which translated means, unconquerable, unalterable, unbreakable, and unrelenting.

When we say an individual is "adamant about something" it means they are iron-willed, determine, firm, steadfast, and tough.

Geologists informs us that the formation of diamonds requires very high temperatures and are formed under an extreme amount of pressure and heat. Life's test, trails, and sufferings bring pressure which gives us endurance to withstand the storms of life.

We are under pressure, but God is controlling the heat. His word is purifying, and He will make you, if you are yielded to His will, a diamond for His glory. Romans 5:3 (esv) *"We rejoice in our sufferings, knowing that suffering produces endurance, and endurance character, and character produces hope, and hope does not put us to shame, because God's love has been poured into our hearts through the Holy Spirit that has been given us."*

Your worth to God is very valuable and you have been a diamond in the rough long enough. Your exceptional characteristics and future potential will no longer be hidden. It is your season to shine, like the sparkle diamond that God has created you to be for His glory and purpose, giving light in a world of darkness. Diamonds give off a reflection and you are God's reflection. Sparkle, Glitter, Twinkle.

It is Destiny Time!

God's Promise for You Today
(Meditate)

Isaiah 62:3 (ESV)

"You shall be a crown of beauty in the hand of the Lord and a royal diadem in the hand of the Lord."

Malachi 3:17 (ESV)

"In that day when I make up my jewels (treasured possession) I will spare them as a man spared his own son that severs him."

1 Peter 2:9 (NIV)

"But you are a chosen people a royal priesthood, a holy nation, God's special possession that you may declare the praises of him who called you of darkness into his wonderful light."

Journal Your Journey

Reflect on your diamond process. Are you still a diamond in the rough? Are you under pressure? Are you in the fire? Is God shaping the many facets of your life? Are you in the final stage and radiating God's light? Write about your diamond journey.

Day 28
You Are God's Diamond for This World

Hannah wanted
a baby. God wanted
a prophet. Align
your vision with
God's purpose!

~ Dr. Bendetta Perry

Day 29

The Birthing of a Promise

*H*annah, whose name means favor and grace, had birthing pains years before she became pregnant with her promise child, whom she named Samuel. Year after year, she journeyed from Jerusalem to Shiloh, the place of worship, with her husband Elkanah, his second wife Peninnah, and their children.

Hannah had no children, and Peninnah would provoke her, miserably by making fun of her, because the Lord had closed her womb. Hannah cried the whole journey and would not eat, because the emptiness in her heart left her feeling worthless due to being barren.

We all have had feelings of worthlessness when we do not measure up to the standards we have set for ourselves or that others have set for us. In Hannah's era, it was a disgrace to be barren. Her husband had the right to take another wife, if she was not able to produce a seed who could receive his inheritance and help build the land that he owned.

Yet, this time, as she took the yearly journey to Shiloh, her life would never be the same. Hannah made up her mind, she was coming to Shiloh to worship God and ignore the spirit in Peninnah, who tortured her with unpleasant words.

God is a spirit, and they that worship Him must worship Him in spirit and truth. Hannah came to Shiloh with a mindset to worship God and lay her petition at His feet. As tears flowed down her eyes and her lips moved with silence, it was there, in front of the entrance of the tabernacle, where she made a vow of promise unto the Lord. If He would look on her affliction and give her a son, she would give her son back to God.

Does God answer all prayers? NO! Which prayers does God answer? The ones that lineup with His will? Exodus 13:2 reads, *"Consecrate to Me all the firstborn, whatever opens the womb among the children of Israel, both of man and beast; it is Mine."*

God gave Hannah a child, because she committed to keep God's Law. Once God knew her heart was aligned with His will, God knew He could trust her to keep her word.

Hannah wanted a son and God wanted a prophet. God held Hanna's womb closed until the right time to replace Eli and his corrupt son's. God chose her for her character and righteous heart. Have you made a promise to God? Are you willing to keep it? Will God answer your righteous prayer? Remember, God watches over His word to perform it.

<u>God's Promise for You Today</u>
(Meditate)

Mark 11:24 (NIV)
"Therefore, I tell you, whatever you ask for in prayer, believe that you have received it, and it will be yours."

Psalm 37:4-5 (NIV)
"Delight yourself in the Lord and he will give you the desires of your heart, commit your way to the Lord; trust in him and he will do this."

1 Samuel 1:27 (NIV)
"I prayed for this child, and the Lord has granted me what I asked of him."

Journal Your Journey

God chose Hannah for her character and righteous heart. Have you made a promise to God? Are you willing to keep it? Will God answer your righteous prayer? Is God calling you to make adjustment in your character to align with His Will? Complete a heart check and journal your results?

Day 29
The Birthing of a Promise

Day 29
The Birthing of a Promise

_____

_____

_____

_____

_____

_____

_____

_____

_____

_____

_____

_____

_____

_____

_____

_____

_____

_____

_____

_____

_____

_____

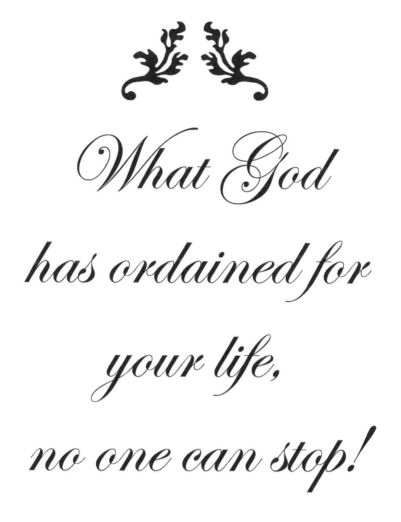

*What God
has ordained for
your life,
no one can stop!*

~ Dr. Bendetta Perry

Day 30

Be Careful Who You Share Your Dreams With

od gives dreams to reveal and communicate His will for our lives. We were all born with a purpose and a destiny to fulfill. Joseph, the son of Jacob, was a gifted dreamer and was also able to interpret the dreams of others.

Joseph was loved by his father more than all his brothers. His father gave him a beautiful coat of many colors. Joseph had a favorable dream, that he told to his brothers, and they hated him all the more. He said to them, *"Listen to this dream I had. We were binding sheaves of grain out in the field, when suddenly my sheaf rose and stood upright, while your sheaves gathered around mine and bowed down to it."*

His brothers said to him, *"Do you intend to reign over us? Will you actually rule us?"* They hated him all the more because of his dream and what he had said. In the moment his brothers responded, they spoke words of indignation towards him.

Yet, Joseph told his brothers his second dream. *"Listen,"* he said, *"I had another dream, and this time the sun, and moon, and eleven stars were bowing down to me."*

When he told his father, as well as his brothers, his father rebuked him and said, *"What is this dream you had? Will your mother, and I, and your bothers actually come and bow down to the ground before you?"*

Everyone, and sometimes family, cannot handle the vision or dream God has given you concerning your future. If you tell your dream too soon, and without God's permission, people will use their tongue of doubt and unbelief to try and abort the dream, that God would use you for His Glory.

Has God placed a dream in your heart? You may be wondering why it has not come to pass yet. Perhaps you shared it with the wrong person, and they spoke against it, leaving you to doubt what God showed you it secret.

I am reminded of a scripture in the book of Habakkuk 2:3, *"For the vision is yet for an appointed time, but at the end it shall speak, and not lie: though it tarry, wait for it; because it will surely come, it will not tarry."*

Joseph was sold into slavery by his brothers for 20 pieces of silver. They lied to Jacob and told him Joseph was killed by a wild animal. Many years passed and Joseph went through many trails and victories as a slave, even being put in a prison; yet, everywhere Joseph was positioned, God prospered him and those around him.

Pharaoh, the ruler of Egypt, had a dream. Only Joseph, the slave, could interpret the dream. Immediately Pharaoh said to Joseph, *"I hereby put you in charge of the entire land of Egypt."*

There was famine in Egypt, and everyone had to come and bow down before Joseph, who was in charge of the distribution of the food and all the land. Joseph's brothers were sent by their father, Jacob, to go to Egypt and buy food. It was there, they bowed before Joseph, the second in command of Egypt, and the brother they sold into slavery, trying to abort the dream which was being fulfilled before their very eyes.

Praise God! Singing out of my heart, the promises of God. *"Whatever God has for me; it is for me! Whatever God has for me; it is for me! I know without a doubt, God will bring me out."*

Beloved help me sing that song, because the promises of God are for you, your children, their children, and all that believe.

God's Promise for You Today
(Meditate)

Genesis 40:8 (NIV)

"We both had dreams, "they answered, but there is no one to interpret them. Then Joseph said to them, "Do not interpretations belong to God? Tell me your dreams."

Numbers 12:6 (NIV)

He said: "Listen to my words: "When there is a prophet among you, I, the LORD, reveal myself to them in visions, I speak to them in dreams."

Matthew 2:13 (NIV)

"When they had gone, an angel of the Lord appeared to Joseph in a dream. "Get up, "he said, take the child and his mother and escape to Egypt. Stay there until I tell you, for Herod is going to search for the child to kill him."

Journal Your Journey

Has God placed a dream in your heart?
Are you wondering why it has not come
to pass yet? Start by writing out your
dream. Recall the promises that God
made to you. Next, cancel ever negative or
doubtful thoughts and words spoken over
your dream, and loose the breath of life
on your dream, by declaring God's word.

_____

_____

_____

_____

_____

_____

_____

_____

_____

_____

_____

_____

_____

_____

_____

_____

_____

_____

_____

_____

_____

_____

Life without Christ is like receiving a rose with no fragrance. Be the one rose that releases a sweet-smelling aroma.

~ Dr. Bendetta Perry

Day 31

God's Flower Garden

*B*eautiful, gorgeous, sweet-smelling, colorful flowers are blooming everywhere. You are part of the aromatic scent from God's flower garden, releasing the sweet aroma of Christ in everyplace God has planted you to bloom; helping others grow into beautiful flowers by the watering of the word of God, love, and encouragement in their lives.

Your fragrance is like perfume, that causes those who encounter your aroma to say, *"Excuse me, what fragrance are you wearing?"* How many times have we heard or asked someone this same question? I just love it when I am asked about the perfume I have on, especially when I am not wearing any perfume, it's the aroma of Christ.

Flowers have a sweet pleasant smell that attracts us to their scent and beauty. The scent that God has given us to release as flowers in His garden is love, joy, peace, patience, kindness, goodness, faithfulness, gentleness, and self-control towards one another. Our scent is watering the garden with the character of God, which is His word flowing through you to others.

Your fragrance is a sweet-smelling perfume unto the Lord and once it is released in the atmosphere it will demolish any works of the flesh: gossip, lies, jealousy, outbursts of anger, uncleanness, selfish ambition, hatred, backbiting, unforgiveness, hate, and other sins, and can alter the atmosphere to a Christ-like pleasantness.

Allow God to cultivate your heart with His love and become a beautiful flower in God's Flower Garden.

God's Promise for You Today
(Meditate)

Galatians 5:22-24 (NIV)

"But the fruit of the Spirit is love, joy, peace, patience, kindness, goodness, faithfulness, gentleness and self-control. Against such things there is no law. Those who belong to Christ Jesus have crucified the sinful nature with its passions and desires. Since we live by the spirit, let us keep in step with the Spirit. Let us not become conceited, provoking and envying each other.

2 Corinthians 2:14-15 (NIV)

"But thanks be to God, who always leads us in triumphal procession in Christ and through us spreads everywhere the fragrance of the knowledge of him. For we are to God the aroma of Christ among those who are being saved and those who are perishing. To the one we are the smell of death; to the other, the fragrance of life.

Ephesians 5:2 (NIV)

"Be imitators to God, therefore, as dearly loved children and live a life of love, just as Christ loved us and gave himself up for us as a fragrant offering and sacrifice to God."

Journal Your Journey

What perfume are you wearing? Which refreshing scent of the Fruit of the Spirit are you covered in today? Write your experience of being asked, "What perfume you are wearing," but it was actually the essence of God.

Day 31
God's Flower Garden

My Prayer for You

Thank you, for taking this 31 Day Journey with me through the Promises of God. I pray that you have been inspired, encouraged, and strengthened in your faith; to believe God for every promise in His Word. God will never abandon, leave, or forsake you. He is faithful to His Word to perform it. The Lord will perfect that which concerns you. Your mercy, O Lord, endures Forever; You will not forsake the works of Your hand!

Amen.

Dr. Bendetta Perry

Made in the
USA
Middletown, DE